SCHIRMER'S LIBRARY
OF MUSICAL CLASSICS

Vol. 832

IGNACE PLEYEL

Op.

T0078854

Six Little Duets
For Two Violins

Arranged for Violin and Piano
(or for Two Violins and Piano)

The Piano Accompaniment by
FRIEDRICH HERMANN

G. SCHIRMER, Inc.

DISTRIBUTED BY

HAL•LEONARD®
CORPORATION
7777 W. BLUEMOUND RD. P.O. BOX 13819 MILWAUKEE, WI 53213

Duo I.

I. Pleyel. Op. 8.

Printed in the U. S. A.

Tempo di Menuetto.

Duo II.

Duo III.

Duo IV.

Violin I

SCHIRMER'S LIBRARY
OF MUSICAL CLASSICS

Vol. 832

IGNACE PLEYEL

Op. 8

Six Little Duets
For Two Violins

Arranged for Violin and Piano
(or for Two Violins and Piano)

The Piano Accompaniment by
FRIEDRICH HERMANN

G. SCHIRMER, *Inc.*

DISTRIBUTED BY
HAL•LEONARD®
CORPORATION
7777 W. BLUEMOUND RD. P.O. BOX 13819 MILWAUKEE, WI 53213

Duo I.

Violino Primo.

⊓: Down-bow.
Ⅴ: Up-bow.

I. PLEYEL. Op. 8.

Allegro moderato.

Printed in the U. S. A.

Violino Primo.

Tempo di Menuetto.

Duo II.
Violino Primo.

Rondo.
Allegretto.

Duo III.

Violino Primo.

Andantino grazioso.

Duo IV.

Violino Primo.

Violino Primo.

Romance.

Rondo.
Allegretto.

Duo V.

Violino Primo.

Violino Primo.

Duo VI.

Violino Primo.

Romance.
Andante.

Allegro.

Romanze.
Andante.

Andante.

attacca

Rondo.
Allegretto.

Duo V.

Duo VI.

Romance.
Andante.